First Encyclopedia of Seas & Oceans

Ben Denne

Designed by Nelupa Hussain
and Helen Wood

Illustrated by David Hancock

Consultants: Dr. Margaret Rostron, Dr. John Rostron,
John Davidson and H.M. Hignett

Usborne Quicklinks

The Usborne Quicklinks Website is packed with links to the best websites on the internet. For links and downloadable pictures for this book, go to:

www.usborne-quicklinks.com
and enter the keywords **"first seas"**

You'll find links to websites where you can:

- Take a journey to the bottom of the ocean
- Watch videos of sea creatures in their habitats
- Search for sunken treasure
- Test your knowledge with undersea quizzes

Downloadable pictures
You can download lots of the pictures in this book and use them in your projects. All the pictures marked with a ★ are available to download at the Usborne Quicklinks Website.

Internet safety guidelines
When using the internet please follow the internet safety guidelines displayed on the Usborne Quicklinks Website.

Contents

4 Seas and oceans
6 Underwater life
8 Who eats who?
10 Hiding
12 Coral reefs
14 Coral reef animals
16 Living together
18 Poisonous animals
20 Sharks
22 Rays
24 Whales
26 Dolphins
28 Deep sea
30 On the move
32 Cold oceans
34 Waves
36 Currents
37 Tides
38 Coasts
40 Seashore life
42 Dangerous seas
44 Boats and ships
46 Exploring the depths
47 Unknown seas

48 Shipwrecks
50 Using the oceans
52 Dirty oceans
54 Emptying the oceans
56 Getting warmer
58 The future of the oceans
60 Undersea facts and records
62 Index

Seas and oceans

More than two-thirds of the Earth is covered with salty water. This makes the planet look blue from space.

The water is divided into five large areas called oceans. In some places these are divided into smaller areas called seas.

Watery world

It is like a different world under the oceans. There are deep valleys, huge mountains, forests of seaweed and many amazing sea animals.

Internet links

For links to websites with games and activities about the ocean, go to **www.usborne-quicklinks.com** and type in the keywords "first seas".

Coast

Oil platform

Divers only go down to about 150m (500ft). The deepest parts of the oceans may be more than 80 times deeper than this.

Most oceans have a shallow area near the coast.

Oil gets trapped between layers of rock under the sea.

At the bottom of the sea is the seabed.

People drill holes into the seabed to get the oil out. See page 51 to find out more.

Arctic Ocean

North America

Europe

Asia

Atlantic Ocean

Africa

Pacific Ocean

Pacific Ocean

The Pacific is the biggest ocean. It covers almost a third of the Earth.

South America

Indian Ocean

Australia

Southern Ocean

This map shows the five different oceans. Remember that the world is round, so the two parts of the Pacific Ocean join up.

Some islands are the tops of enormous undersea mountains.

Darkest depths

The deepest place in any ocean is the Mariana Trench in the Pacific. If you dropped a 1kg (2.2lb) rock into the water there, it would take over an hour to reach the seabed.

Undersea volcanoes throw out boiling melted rock called lava.

The 88-floor Petronas Towers in Malaysia are among the world's tallest buildings. Even 28 of them stood one on top of the other in the Mariana Trench wouldn't quite reach the water's surface.

The bottoms of deep trenches are completely dark, but some animals live down there.

Underwater life

The oceans are full of living things. Some sea creatures are gentle and friendly, but others are fierce hunters.

Internet links

For links to websites where you can find out all about life underwater, go to **www.usborne-quicklinks.com** and type in the keywords "first seas".

Most types of shark are deadly hunters. They have sharp teeth for eating other animals.

Dolphins are one of the most intelligent and playful kinds of sea animal.

Coral reefs are beautiful underwater structures. They are home to many different sea animals.

Sea slugs collect other animals' poison and use it themselves against their enemies.

What are fish?

Fish are a group of animals that live in water. There are thousands of different kinds. They come in different shapes and sizes, but they all have gills and fins. Gills allow them to breathe under water, and fins help them to move around.

Most fish have flat tails, which they move from side to side to swim. Their strong tail muscles make swimming easy.

Caudal fin

Fish use these top fins, called dorsal fins, to help keep their balance.

This flap, called the operculum, covers the fish's gills.

Pelvic fins help fish to change direction quickly.

Fish use these fins, called pectoral fins, for turning.

This line, called the lateral line, helps fish to sense movement in the water.

Slimy skin helps fish to move easily through water.

★

Breathing

Fish breathe by taking oxygen out of the water. Here's how they do it.

Gills under here

★

★

As a fish moves forward, it takes in water through its mouth. The water passes over its gills.

The fish's gills take oxygen from the water. The water then passes out under the fish's operculum.

Fish scales

Most fish are protected by a covering of tiny plates, called scales. These scales are waterproof, and help to protect the fish from pests and hunters.

Fish scales overlap each other, to make a protective cover.

★

★

The rings on a fish's scales show how old the fish is. Some fish can live for up to 80 years.

7

Who eats who?

The animals in the oceans depend on each other to survive. Some animals eat plants, but some hunt and eat other animals.

Hunters and hunted

Animals which hunt and eat other animals are known as predators. The animals that they eat are called prey.

This killer whale is a predator. It is hunting mackerel. The mackerel are its prey.

Drifting plankton

Plankton are animals and plants which provide food for lots of other animals. There are billions of them in the oceans. They cannot swim, so they drift through the water. Most kinds of plankton are tiny.

Tiny plants in the water, such as these diatoms, are called phytoplankton.

One glass of sea water can contain as many as 50,000 phytoplankton.

These zooplankton animals are shown larger than they really are. In real life, most of them are actually smaller than one of the letters in these words.

Web of life

Food webs, like this one, show who eats who. The arrows point from the prey to the predators. Most predators are also prey for other, bigger animals. Predators which aren't eaten by other animals are called top predators.

Which are the top predators in this web?

Killer whale ★

Humpback whale ★

Tuna ★

Herring ★

Mackerel ★

Zooplankton ★

Phytoplankton ★

New from old

When animals are eaten by other animals, they pass on energy. Even if they die of old age, the energy is still passed on through the food web. When they die, animals help create new life. Follow the numbers to see how this happens.

①

4. Plankton use the nutrients to build their bodies, which sea animals eat before they die.

④

1. When a sea animal dies, it sinks to the seabed and gets covered in mud.

②

③

3. Bacteria break the remains down into separate parts called nutrients, and release them back into the water.

2. In the mud are tiny living things called bacteria. They feed on the remains of the dead animal.

Internet links

For links to websites where you can find out more about food webs, go to **www.usborne-quicklinks.com**.

9

Hiding

Many sea animals are difficult to spot because the patterns on their bodies look like their surroundings. This is called camouflage. Camouflage helps animals to hide when they are in danger. It can also help predators sneak up on prey.

Sea dragons have lots of leafy parts on their bodies, to make them look like seaweed.

Wobbegong sharks have flat bodies. They lie on the seabed, and snap up fish that swim past.

Flatfish disguise

Some flatfish use the seabed for camouflage. They cover themselves in sand and lie very still so they won't be seen.

Can you see the fish in this picture?

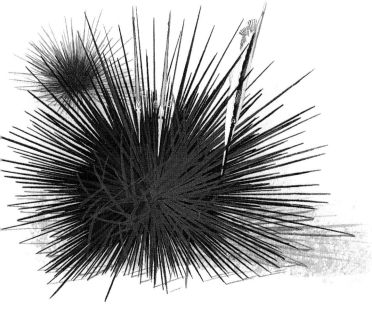

Safe spines

Shrimpfish hide by hanging head-down among the spines of sea urchins. The stripes along the sides of their bodies make them look like one of the sea urchin's spines. This protects them from predators.

Can you see the shrimpfish hiding on this sea urchin?

Changing patterns

Cuttlefish hunt on the seabed, eating fish and crabs. They have long tentacles which dart out to catch their prey. As they pass over different areas, their body pattern changes completely, to match their surroundings.

This cuttlefish is camouflaged against the sand.

As it moves over some rocks, its pattern changes.

Fierce frogfish

Sargassum frogfish live in areas of floating sargassum seaweed. Their bodies are perfectly camouflaged to look like the seaweed. They stay very still, and wait for their prey to swim close to them.

A sargassum frogfish can use its front fins like hands to cling to the seaweed.

Coral reefs

Corals live in warm, shallow seas. Although they look like plants, corals are really made of thousands of small animals. Large areas of coral are called coral reefs.

Internet links

For links to websites where you can learn about lots of different kinds of corals, go to **www.usborne-quicklinks.com** and type in the keywords "first seas".

Angelfish live among corals. Their bright markings help them blend in with their background.

Coral animals

Coral animals, called polyps, are protected by hard skeletons. When they die, the skeletons remain and new polyps grow on top of them. Over time, a coral reef slowly forms.

There are four fish and an eel hiding in this coral reef. Can you spot them all?

A coral polyp, cut in half

Poisonous tentacles for catching food

Mouth

Stomach

Stony base

★

Sea fan

Sponge

Sea urchin

Brittle star

Brain coral

Reef life

Coral reefs are full of nooks and crannies where animals can hide and make their homes. This means there are always lots of living things around them.

A coral meal

The animals in coral are well protected by their shells, but some fish, such as parrotfish, are able to eat them.

A parrotfish's teeth are all joined together to form a hard beak.

The parrotfish breaks off a chunk of coral, then uses its beak to crunch it up.

Giant clam

Feather star

Sea anemone

Coral reef animals

More than a quarter of all the creatures in the sea live around coral reefs. This includes animals of all shapes and sizes, and more than 2,000 kinds of fish.

Octopuses can squirt ink into the water if they are attacked. This makes the water cloudy, helping them to escape.

Clown triggerfish swim over the coral eating tiny animals, such as worms, which live on it.

Giant groupers are the biggest coral reef predators. They can grow to the length of a small car.

Internet links

For links to websites where you can do activities about coral reef animals, go to **www.usborne-quicklinks.com** and type in the keywords "first seas".

Angelfish eat sponges, which live on the coral.

Seahorses live among corals. They swim by moving the fin on their backs.

Safe on the reef

Coral reefs are home to fierce predators such as sharks, so reef animals need to have ways of protecting themselves. Some have patterns which make them look scary. Others have stranger tricks.

Boxfish are covered in a foul-tasting slime, which protects them from predators.

Pufferfish blow themselves up when they are frightened, to scare off predators.

Predators may think the spot on this butterfly fish's back is the eye of a really big fish.

Safe in schools

Some fish swim in big groups called schools. This helps confuse predators, so they don't know which fish to attack. They might even think the whole school is a much bigger animal.

These crescent-tailed bigeye fish are swimming close together in a school.

Living together

Some sea creatures need help from other animals to survive. This is called symbiosis. Usually symbiosis is good for both animals, but sometimes it only helps one of them.

Long, thin fish called remoras often cling to bigger animals such as this green turtle. They feed on leftover scraps from the bigger animals' meals.

Living home

Pearlfish use other animals for protection by living inside them. Sometimes they start to eat the animals they live in from the inside.

This pearlfish is living inside a sea cucumber. It gets in and out through the sea cucumber's breathing hole.

Safe from stings

Anemones eat little fish. They have stinging tentacles to kill fish which swim into them. Clownfish live among these tentacles but the poison doesn't harm them. This keeps them safe from enemies, which get stung when they swim too close.

Clownfish are covered in a slime which protects them from the anemone's poison.

Goby watchman

Some kinds of shrimp are nearly blind. These shrimp live with fish called gobies, and the two animals help each other. The shrimp build safe burrows for both animals to live in, and in return the gobies watch out for predators.

A shrimp builds a burrow with its strong claws, which both animals live in.

When they are outside, the shrimp keeps a feeler on the goby's tail.

If the goby senses danger, it swishes its tail. Both animals quickly hide in the burrow.

Pest control

Cleaner fish live on coral reefs. They swim around bigger fish, picking off dead skin and pests. Sometimes bigger fish, such as these groupers, line up to get cleaned. Cleaner fish wriggle their bodies so that the fish they clean recognize them, and don't eat them.

Sometimes bigger fish let cleaner fish into their mouths to clean their teeth and gills.

Underwater dentist

Banded coral shrimp use their long, sharp claws to clean other animals' skin and teeth. They eat the bits of food they find. The bigger animals know they are helping, and don't try to eat them.

This banded coral shrimp is picking bits of food from a moray eel's teeth.

17

Poisonous animals

Some of the most poisonous animals in the world live in the sea. They use poison to catch their prey, or to protect themselves from enemies.

These animals all have deadly poison, and can kill people.

★ Box jellyfish

★ Rabbitfish

★ Portuguese man-of-war

★ Stonefish

★ Cone shell

Lionfish are covered with spines, which are filled with poison.

Small but deadly

The blue-ringed octopus has a deadly poison in its bite which stops its prey from breathing. Blue-ringed octopus bites have even killed people.

The bright blue patterns on this blue-ringed octopus warn predators that it is poisonous.

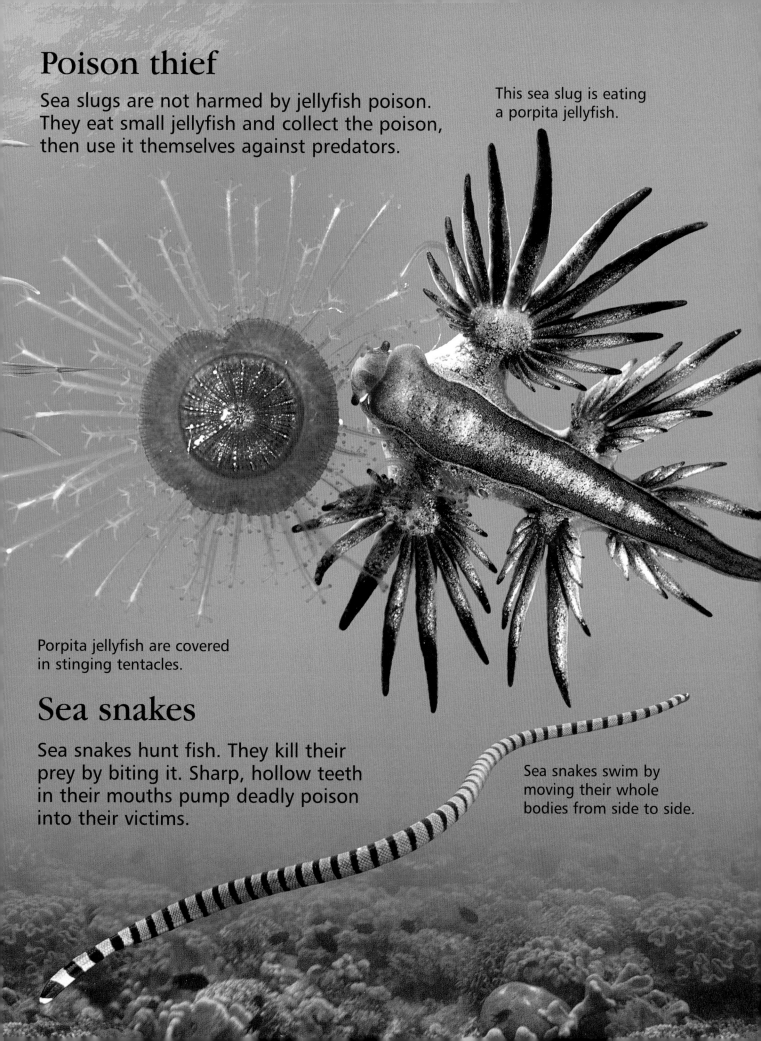

Poison thief

Sea slugs are not harmed by jellyfish poison. They eat small jellyfish and collect the poison, then use it themselves against predators.

This sea slug is eating a porpita jellyfish.

Porpita jellyfish are covered in stinging tentacles.

Sea snakes

Sea snakes hunt fish. They kill their prey by biting it. Sharp, hollow teeth in their mouths pump deadly poison into their victims.

Sea snakes swim by moving their whole bodies from side to side.

Sharks

Sharks are fish which live in oceans all over the world. There are more than 300 different kinds. Most are fierce hunters, with sharp teeth for catching and killing other animals.

Internet links

For links to websites with lots of shark activities, go to **www.usborne-quicklinks.com** and type in the keywords "first seas".

Whale sharks are not a danger to people. Divers can swim with them safely.

Great white shark

People killers?

Great white sharks like to surprise their prey from below and kill it with only one bite, to save energy. They sometimes attack swimmers, but scientists believe they do this by mistake, thinking that humans are other sea animals.

Great white sharks kill their prey by biting it. They can open their mouths very wide.

As their mouths open, their teeth point forward, helping them to take a bigger bite.

Whale sharks are the world's biggest fish. They can grow up to 12m (40ft) long.

Hammerhead sharks have eyes on each end of a long, flat head. This helps them to see all around as they swim.

Sharks swim by moving their tails from side to side.

Fin shapes

Sharks, like dolphins and whales, sometimes swim near the surface of the sea with their dorsal (back) fins sticking out of the water. Dorsal fins of different animals look different, as you can see below.

A common dolphin has a small, gently curved fin.

A great white shark's fin is sharp and triangular.

The fin of a killer whale can be as tall as a person.

Hundreds of teeth

Most sharks have at least three rows of teeth. As they lose the ones in front, teeth from the rows behind move forward to replace them.

A sand tiger shark's teeth point back so that fish it catches can't wriggle free.

Rays

There are hundreds of different kinds of rays. They all have flat bodies. Some are harmless, but stingrays can give a poisonous sting from their tails and electric rays can give an electric shock. They do this to protect themselves if they are attacked.

You can see the poisonous spine on the end of this stingray's tail.

Organs on the sides of an electric ray's head can give a powerful shock.

These huge manta rays are swimming in a school.

Feeding

Most rays have their mouths on the underneath of their bodies. They swim along the seabed, eating things they swim over and can crunch up shells with their teeth to get to the animals inside.

This picture shows the underneath of a ray. The position of its mouth helps it to feed on the seabed.

Mouth

Gills

Internet links

For links to websites where you can find out all about rays, go to **www.usborne-quicklinks.com** and type in the keywords "first seas".

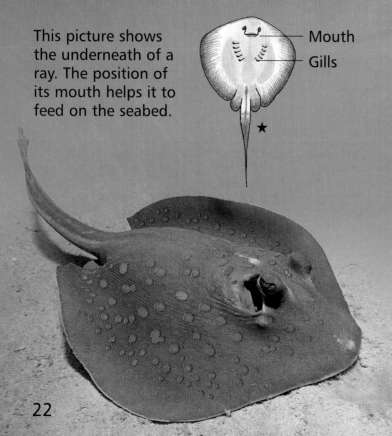

Stingrays move along the seabed by rippling their fins.

22

Manta rays

The biggest kinds of rays are manta rays. They can be up to 6m (20ft) across, but are not dangerous. They feed by swimming slowly with their mouths open, eating plankton and other tiny animals floating in the water.

These flaps, called cephalic lobes, help to push food into the ray's mouth.

Divers sometimes swim with manta rays. You can find out about diving on page 48.

Manta rays swim by moving their fins up and down, like enormous wings.

Whales

Whales are the biggest animals in the world. They look like fish, but whales are actually mammals. Unlike most mammals though, whales do not have hair on their bodies.

This sperm whale is as heavy as six elephants. The heaviest animals on Earth are blue whales, which can weigh as much as 20 elephants.

Spout shapes

Mammals can't breathe under water, so whales come to the ocean's surface to breathe. They breathe through holes called blowholes on top of their heads. When they breathe out, they shoot out sprays of water. This is called spouting.

Different whales spout in different ways. By looking at the shape of a whale's spout, you can tell what kind of whale it is.

Humpback whale

Blue whale

Right whale

Sperm whale

Minke whale

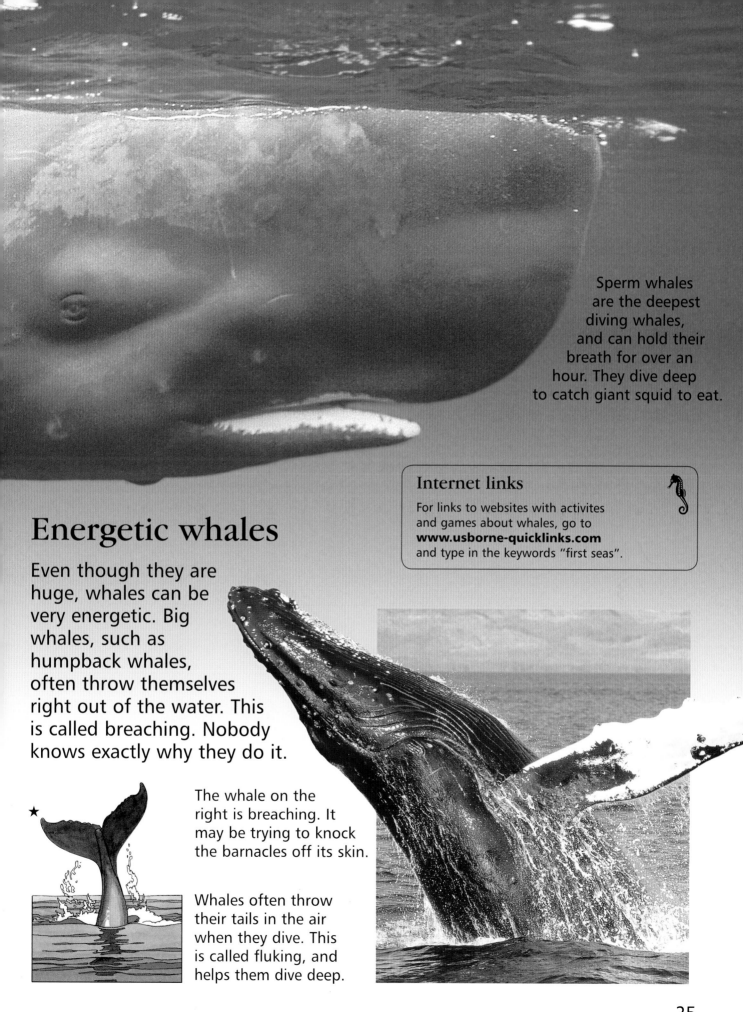

Sperm whales are the deepest diving whales, and can hold their breath for over an hour. They dive deep to catch giant squid to eat.

Energetic whales

Even though they are huge, whales can be very energetic. Big whales, such as humpback whales, often throw themselves right out of the water. This is called breaching. Nobody knows exactly why they do it.

Internet links

For links to websites with activites and games about whales, go to **www.usborne-quicklinks.com** and type in the keywords "first seas".

The whale on the right is breaching. It may be trying to knock the barnacles off its skin.

Whales often throw their tails in the air when they dive. This is called fluking, and helps them dive deep.

Dolphins

Dolphins are mammals that live in oceans all over the world. They often live in big groups. They are some of the most intelligent animals in the sea.

A group of dolphins is called a school. Some schools contain over a hundred dolphins.

Internet links

For links to websites where you can find answers to all your questions about dolphins, go to **www.usborne-quicklinks.com** and type in the keywords "first seas".

Learning to breathe

Dolphins breathe air, so when a baby dolphin is born, its mother must quickly push it to the surface of the sea and teach it to breathe, or else it will drown. Sometimes, another dolphin helps her do this.

★ This dolphin has just had a baby. Now the baby must learn how to breathe.

★ The mother swims under her baby, and gently pushes it up.

★ The baby takes its first breath of air. Later, it will know what to do.

Dolphins can swim
at speeds of up to
40kph (25mph).

Fun and games

Dolphins are fast swimmers and
amazing acrobats. Their speed helps
them catch fish, but they also love
to play and perform tricks. They
can jump right out of the sea.

Spinner dolphins can jump up to
3m (10ft) out of the water, and
spin around as many as
seven times in the air.

These bottlenose dolphins
are taking a look around.
This is called spy hopping.

Using echoes

Dolphins find their way in the
sea by making sounds which
send back echoes. They can
then tell what's around them
by listening to the echoes.
This is called sonar. Dolphins
also use sonar to catch fish.

A dolphin
makes a clicking
sound which
travels through
the water.

When the
sound hits
some fish, it
bounces back
as an echo.

The dolphin
can tell where
the fish are by
listening to the
returning echo.

27

The deep sea is a very dark, cold place where some of the strangest creatures in the world live. There are no plants in the deep sea, so all the fish are hunters.

Hatchetfish have eyes on top of their heads so they can see fish which swim above them.

Internet links

For links to websites where you can find out more about the deep sea, go to **www.usborne-quicklinks.com**.

Gulper eels have enormous mouths. They can eat animals which are much larger than themselves.

Vampire squid

Vampire squid live as deep as 900m (3,000ft). Their big eyes help them see in the murky depths.

Vampire squid have a clever way of escaping from enemies. They can turn themselves inside out. The undersides of their tentacles are covered in sharp spikes, to stop other animals from eating them.

Vampire squid escape from enemies by putting their tentacles over their heads.

Their tentacles cover their bodies, making a spiky shield which protects them.

Seeing in the dark

Because it is so dark at the bottom of the oceans, some fish have ways of making light to help them see. Light also attracts other sea animals, so some hunters use it to catch food.

Lanternfish have lights on their bodies to confuse enemies.

Viperfish have spots of light all the way along their bodies.

Flashlight fish have a light just below their eyes. They can turn it on and off.

Crinoids may look like plants, but they aren't. They are actually related to starfish.

Hatchetfish

Anglerfish have a light hanging over their mouths.

Fish are attracted by the anglerfish's light, and swim right into its mouth.

On the move

Some sea animals have to make long journeys. They do this to find food, or to give birth. It is called migrating.

Wandering whales

Some whales migrate to the cold oceans in summer because the water there is full of krill, a kind of plankton which they can eat. In winter, they return to the warmer oceans to have their babies.

Humpback whales

Humpback whales migrate. Some of them travel more that 16,000km (10,000 miles) every year.

The arrows on this map show how far humpback whales travel each year.

Summer   Winter

Up and down

Some sea animals migrate every day. Copepods are a kind of plankton which stay in the deep sea during the day, but swim up to the surface at night to feed.

Copepods

This copepod is shown larger than it really is. Copepods are actually difficult to see, because they are so small.

Turtle travels

When she is ready to lay eggs, a female turtle goes back to the beach where she was born.

She makes a hole in the sand with her flippers. She lays her eggs in it and covers them with sand.

7 to 10 weeks later, baby turtles hatch from the eggs. They make their way down to the sea.

Years later, when they are fully grown, the female turtles return to the same beach to lay their own eggs.

Eel adventures

Freshwater eels live in rivers until they are ready to lay eggs. Then they swim to the Sargasso Sea in the middle of the Atlantic Ocean to lay their eggs and die.

Baby eels, called elvers, swim back to the river that their parents came from. This can take as long as three years.

Internet links

For links to websites with turtle games and activities, go to **www.usborne-quicklinks.com** and type in the keywords "first seas".

Salmon journeys

Salmon spend their lives in the ocean, but they always return to the part of the river where they were born to lay eggs.

Salmon have to swim up rivers and jump up waterfalls to get back to their birthplace.

Cold oceans

The Arctic and Southern oceans are always cold. The surface of these oceans is frozen for most of the year, but the water under the ice is full of life.

Antarctic icefish have special liquid in their blood, to stop it from freezing.

★

Icy problem

Weddell seals hunt for food under the ice, but they have to come to the surface to breathe.

This Weddell seal has made a breathing hole through the ice.

It scrapes at the ice with its sharp teeth, to keep the hole open.

Walruses

Walruses are mammals that live on land and in the sea. They eat clams, which live on the seabed. A layer of fatty blubber under their skins keeps them warm.

Internet links

For links to websites where you can play games and try activities about the Arctic and Antarctica, go to **www.usborne-quicklinks.com**

Walruses have big teeth called tusks. These male walruses are using their tusks to fight each other.

Penguins

Seven different kinds of penguins live in the Antarctic. Lots of birds could not live in such a cold and icy place, but penguins have found ways of surviving the freezing conditions.

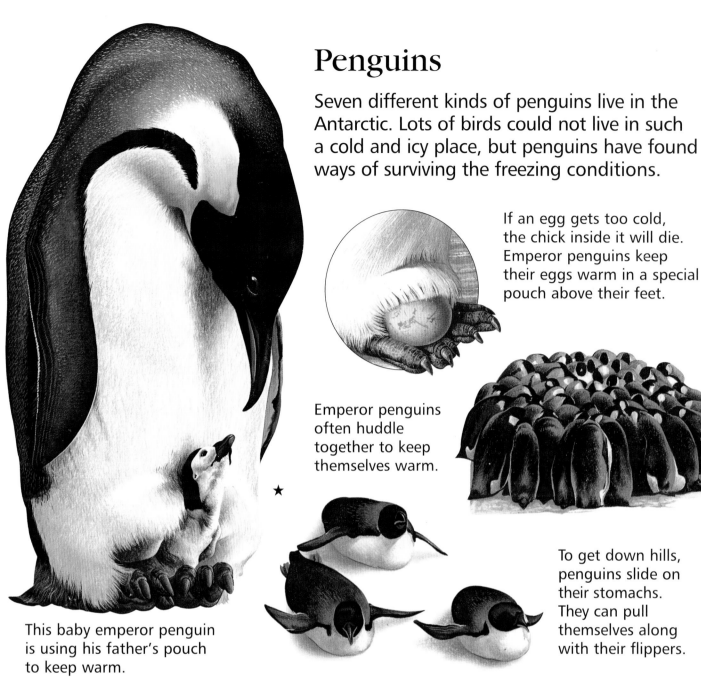

If an egg gets too cold, the chick inside it will die. Emperor penguins keep their eggs warm in a special pouch above their feet.

Emperor penguins often huddle together to keep themselves warm.

To get down hills, penguins slide on their stomachs. They can pull themselves along with their flippers.

This baby emperor penguin is using his father's pouch to keep warm.

Strong swimmers

Penguins cannot fly, but they are very good swimmers and can stay underwater for up to 18 minutes. They catch krill, fish and squid to eat.

Penguins jump or dive into the sea from the ice.

Penguins use their webbed feet to swim fast underwater.

Penguins often jump out of the water to take a breath.

Sometimes they swim along the surface of the water, like ducks.

Waves

Waves are made far out at sea by the wind. They sometimes travel enormous distances across the oceans before finally crashing onto the seashore.

This picture shows what the different parts of a wave are called.

Making waves

Wind blowing across the sea makes ripples on the water. If the wind continues to blow, the ripples will get bigger and bigger, until they turn into waves.

When the wind blows across the top of waves it creates foam on them and makes them grow.

Breaking waves

The shape of a wave is affected by the depth of the sea. This makes waves change shape as they get closer to the coast.

Internet links

For links to websites with activities about waves, go to **www.usborne-quicklinks.com** and type in the keywords "first seas".

As a wave gets closer to land, the water gets shallower. The bottom part of the wave starts to drag on the seabed and slows down.

The top of the wave now moves faster than the bottom. This makes the top of the wave fall forward and topple over. This is called breaking.

Underwater energy

Waves are a kind of energy, moving through the water. Although the wave moves through the water, the water actually stays in the same place.

If you watch a wave, it looks as if the water moves along, but it doesn't.

When a wave passes under something such as a seagull, it just lifts it up.

When the wave has passed, the seagull is still in the same place as it was before.

Monster waves

The size of a wave depends on how strongly the wind is blowing and the distance it has covered. During storms at sea, strong winds create huge, powerful waves, which are big enough to sink a ship.

In some places, waves can be over 12m (40ft) high. That's higher than a two-floor house.

Currents

Currents are like big rivers which flow through the oceans. Different currents flow at different speeds. Some only move 10km (7 miles) a day. Others move up to 160km (100 miles) a day.

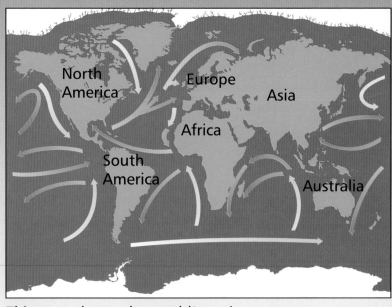

North America

Europe

Asia

Africa

South America

Australia

This map shows the world's main currents.

 Warm current   Cold current

Carried by currents

Plant seeds are sometimes carried a very long way by a current. The new plant can grow a long distance away from its parent.

Internet links

For links to websites where you can find out more about currents and tides, go to **www.usborne-quicklinks.com** and type in the keywords "first seas".

Plant seeds, such as this coconut, fall in the sea. The current carries them away.

The seed sometimes travels for long distances before nearing land.

Waves carry the seed onto the shore, where it may put down roots and grow.

Tides

The height of the sea is called sea level. The sea level in most places is constantly changing through the day as the sea moves up and down the beach. This movement is called the tide.

Tides sometimes come in very fast and trap people on beaches.

Tidelines

When the water reaches its highest point on a beach, it leaves a line of things from the sea behind. Then it starts to move back down the beach again. This line is called a tideline.

Seagulls look through tidelines, eating pieces of food they find.

There is often lots of seaweed left behind when the tide goes out.

The bones of cuttlefish, called cuttlebones, are often washed up on beaches by the tide.

This is a dogfish egg case. It is called a mermaid's purse.

Coasts

Coasts are the places where the land meets the sea. Coasts are always changing shape as waves and the wind wear them away.

Waves throw pebbles and rocks against the coast. Over time, this wears it away.

Bigger stones are at the back of the beach.

Small stones and sand are near the sea.

Making beaches

Beaches form on low, flat parts of the coast. Waves grind down big rocks and cliffs into smaller stones and pebbles, and finally into sand. Sand often also contains tiny pieces of broken seashells.

Internet links

For links to websites where you can learn more about coasts and sand, go to **www.usborne-quicklinks.com** and type in the keywords "first seas".

Changing coasts

Some parts of a coast are made of harder rock than others. These parts are worn away more slowly by the sea, and form a headland.

Headland

When the top of an arch collapses, a stack or stump is left.

Waves wear away softer rock in the cliffs to make caves.

An arch forms when waves wear away a hole through a headland.

Sorting the stones

The smallest stones on a beach are always the ones nearest to the sea. This is because of breaking waves. As waves crash onto a beach, they slowly sort the stones into different sizes. Here is how it happens:

★ As waves break, they throw pebbles and stones onto the beach.

★ As the water flows back to sea, it carries little pebbles back with it.

★ The bigger stones and pebbles are left farther up the beach.

39

Seashore life

There are lots of things to spot on the seashore. Every day when the tide goes out, it leaves pools of water trapped among the rocks. Plants and animals make their homes in these pools.

Five-bearded rocklings use feelers around their mouths to find their way.

Shrimp keep the water clean, eating anything they can find.

Butterfish have flat, slippery bodies. This helps them squeeze into gaps in the rocks, to hide from predators.

Blennies have large front fins which they use to change direction quickly in small pools.

Seaweed grows all along the seashore.

Outside skeletons

A crab doesn't have a shell, but it has its skeleton on the outside. The skeleton is called a carapace. When the crab grows too big for its carapace, it wriggles out of it. Then its skin slowly hardens to make a new, bigger carapace.

Crab

Mussels

Upside down

Barnacles cover the rocks along the seashore. They feed by sticking their legs out of the tops of their shells.

Tiny barnacles cling to the rocks in big groups. Their tough shells protect them from danger.

Barnacles open the tops of their shells to feed. Their legs stick out to pick up bits of food in the water.

Internet links

For links to websites where you can try seashore activities, go to **www.usborne-quicklinks.com** and type in the keywords "first seas".

Special air bubbles keep this seaweed floating near the surface of the water, where it is light.

Sea scorpions are fierce predators. Their huge mouths can open wide enough to swallow large prey whole.

Starfish have five arms. If they lose an arm, another one grows in its place.

Hermit crab

Sea urchins have sharp spines on their shells to protect them.

Sea lemons scrape food off the rocks with their tongues.

Strawberry anemones

Limpets

Barnacles

Dog whelk

41

Dangerous seas

The weather at sea changes quickly. Violent storms and huge waves appear suddenly and can cause terrible damage.

Hurricanes

Hurricanes are violent storms which form over warm seas. Some hurricanes are so big they can be seen from space. Black clouds, heavy rain, huge waves and winds moving at speeds of up to 480kph (300mph) make hurricanes terrifying.

Waterspouts stretch from the sea all the way up to the clouds.

This is a picture of a hurricane taken from space. The spot in the middle, called the eye of the hurricane, is completely calm.

Waterspouts

Big storms sometimes pull water from the ocean up into a huge, spinning column called a waterspout. Waterspouts move across the ocean, sucking up anything in their path.

Sometimes waterspouts suck up fish and other sea animals. These drop back into the sea when the waterspout dies down.

Tsunami

Earthquakes make the ground move. When they happen under the sea they shake the seabed.

This sometimes creates big, powerful waves. These waves are called tsunami.

When an earthquake happens under the sea, part of the seabed rises or falls.

The movement of the seabed moves the sea above, making long, low tsunami waves.

The waves move out fast in all directions from the place where they were made.

If tsunami reach the coast, they are squeezed up into huge, tall waves.

Wave of destruction

In the deep ocean, tsunami are not dangerous. They are low waves which may pass under ships without anybody noticing. Tsunami only become enormous when they reach shallow water. Then they break and crash down onto the land, destroying everything in their way.

★ The biggest tsunami ever recorded was over 30m (99ft) high.

Internet links

For links to websites where you can learn more about extreme weather, go to **www.usborne-quicklinks.com** and type in the keywords "first seas".

Boats and ships

Boats were invented thousands of years ago. They help people move things from one place to another, and explore the world around them.

Funnel

Cruise ships are like floating hotels. They sometimes have swimming pools and tennis courts on them. ★

Lifeboats like this can be used in emergencies.

A ship's back is called its stern.

4 propellers push the ship forward.

4 engines power the propellers.

Internet links

For links to websites where you can find out more about boats and ships, go to **www.usborne-quicklinks.com** and type in the keywords "first seas".

First boats

The first boats were small. They were made by hollowing out logs. Later, people built bigger boats and ships.

 ★

The first boats were hollowed-out logs. They were heavy, and hard to use.

 ★

Later, people made lighter boats by stretching animal skins around sticks.

 ★

The first big boats were rowing boats, called galleys. This is a Greek galley.

 ★

Wind power

Sailing ships had lots of huge sails instead of oars. The sails filled up with wind which pushed the ships along. When there was no wind, the ships could not go anywhere.

This kind of sailing ship is called a galleon. Galleons were used about 400 years ago.

The radar mast is used for communication, and to check for other ships in the area.

A ship's front is called its bow.

A ship's bottom is called its keel. It keeps the ship steady in the water.

A ship's body is called its hull.

Ships today

Ships today can be much bigger than the ships of the past. They are used to move things, such as fuel and food, from one place to another all over the world. People also relax on huge cruise ships, such as the one shown above. Small, fast boats are sometimes used for travel.

Oil tankers are ships for carrying oil. They can be over 1km (½ mile) long. Some are so big, people on them use bicycles to get around.

A hovercraft can move very quickly. A big cushion of air underneath it makes it fly just above the surface of the sea.

Exploring the depths

Exploring the deep ocean is difficult, because it is so dark and cold. Scientists sometimes use small submarines, called submersibles, to explore the depths. Below is a submersible called Deep Flight.

This picture shows the Deep Flight submersible in use.

These wings don't move. They keep the submersible steady in the water.

Bottles filled with oxygen allow the pilot to breathe.

Deep Flight gets its power from ten batteries (five along each side).

This part is see-through, so the pilot can look around.

DEEP FLIGHT

Engines, called thrusters, turn the propellers.

Propellers spin around quickly, pushing the submersible forward.

The pilot guides the submersible using these hand controls.

These powerful lights help the pilot to find his way.

Crittercams

Sperm whales dive deep. Scientists have attached special cameras, called crittercams, to some of them, to try to take pictures of deep sea animals.

Crittercams are small and light, and don't hurt the animals they are attached to.

Camera

This suction cup sticks to the whale's skin.

Unknown seas

The oceans are full of surprises. People still haven't explored them completely, and scientists are always finding out new things about the amazing animals that live in them.

Giant squid can grow very large, but not many people have seen them in their habitat. Colossal squid can grow to even bigger sizes.

Coelacanth

Dead or alive?

Scientists thought that coelacanths died out 80 million years ago. Then, in 1938, a fisherman from the port of East London in South Africa caught one. Since then, lots more have been found.

Megamouth

Giant jaws

In 1976, scientists discovered a new kind of shark in the sea near Hawaii. They called it a megamouth because of its enormous mouth.

Sea serpents

Sailors in the past reported seeing huge serpents at sea. These might have been oarfish, which grow to over 7m (25ft) long. Scientists know almost nothing about these fish, which spend most of their time in the depths.

Oarfish

Shipwrecks

Ships which have sunk are called shipwrecks. Some shipwrecks are hundreds of years old. This is a Spanish galleon, which sank more than 400 years ago.

Divers exploring shipwreck

Breathing tank

Mask for seeing underwater

Flippers help the diver swim faster.

This diver is drawing the wreck using waterproof paper, and a pen which works underwater.

Exploring shipwrecks

Divers often explore shipwrecks. They wear tanks on their backs, filled with air. They breathe the air through a tube. This means they can stay underwater for a long time.

Sea animals, such as this moray eel, make their homes in nooks and crannies in the wreck.

These divers have found a cannon on the galleon. They are taking it up to the surface using special balloons filled with air.

Artifacts

Man-made things found in shipwrecks are called artifacts. Artifacts often help us learn about how people lived in the past.

These urns come from a wreck in Turkey. The wreck is more than 1,000 years old.

These gold bars were found on a sunken galleon called the *Santa Margerita*.

Internet links

For links to websites where you can discover more about shipwrecks, go to **www.usborne-quicklinks.com** and type in the keywords "first seas"

Over time, coral and plants grow on shipwrecks. This makes them difficult to find.

Some ships carrying treasure have been wrecked. Lots of the treasure has never been found.

This is a plate from the *Titanic*, which sank in 1912 when it hit an iceberg.

Using the oceans

The oceans are very important to us in many ways. We need them to help us survive. We get food and energy from them. They also give us minerals and medicines.

These fishermen in India are throwing out their nets. They hope to catch some fish in them.

Big nets

Fishermen use nets of various sizes to catch fish. Some, like the one above, can only catch a few fish at a time. The huge nets pulled by ships can catch thousands at once. These nets are up to 2km (a mile) long.

Drift nets hang from the surface. They trap fish that try to swim through them.

Purse seine nets are like big bags. They catch herring and other fish near the surface.

Trawl nets drag along the seabed. They catch fish such as plaice that live on the bottom.

Drilling for oil

In some of the rocks under the seabed, there is lots of oil. Big companies use oil platforms to drill holes into the seabed and get it out. It is used as fuel for things such as cars, factories and power stations.

Internet links

To find out more about using the oceans, go to **www.usborne-quicklinks.com** and type in the keywords "first seas".

★ Floating oil platform

These floats stop the platform from sinking.

Cables with anchors on them stop the platform from moving.

Seabed

This pipe goes into the seabed as far as the oil. The oil is then pumped up.

Oil

Food, jewels and medicines

We get a lot more than just food and energy from the oceans. Here are some of the other things that come from the sea.

Mother-of-pearl covers the inside of abalone shells. It is used to decorate things. ★

Pearls are found inside animals called oysters. They are used to make necklaces and earrings. ★

Some kinds of seaweed are good to eat. Seaweed is also used to make shampoo and ice cream. ★

Some medicines come from the sea. Horseshoe crabs' blood is used to test for diseases. ★

51

Dirty oceans

The oceans are getting dirtier and dirtier because of things people dump in them. Our waste kills sea plants and animals. Here are some of the different ways people harm the oceans.

In some places, sewage pipes take waste from bathrooms and toilets and dump it into the sea.

Many farmers use chemicals to help their crops grow. When it rains, some of the chemicals are washed into rivers, and then into the sea.

Plastic dumped in the sea can take longer than 80 years to rot away.

Some ships dump their litter into the sea.

Some people leave litter behind on beaches. When the tide comes in, it is washed out to sea.

Oil spills

Huge oil tankers sometimes hit rocks or crash into other ships and oil leaks out into the sea. This can harm the sea and the animals that live in it.

Internet links

For links to websites where you can learn more about threats to the oceans, go to **www.usborne-quicklinks.com** and type in the keywords "first seas".

Seabirds get oil stuck in their feathers. When they try to clean it off with their beaks, it poisons them.

Some spilled oil floats on top of the water.

Oil tankers carry enormous amounts of oil. A big oil spill can cover a huge area.

When oil washes up on beaches, it sticks to the sand and pebbles and kills the plants and animals along the seashore.

Cleaning up

Cleaning up after an oil spill is a difficult job. People have to catch and clean the oily animals. Then they release them away from the oil.

This oil-covered seal is being cleaned with dishwashing liquid.

53

Emptying the oceans

As well as making the oceans dirty, we damage them in other ways. When we take too much from the oceans, it puts the animals and plants that live in them in danger.

Overfishing

When fishermen catch too many of the same kind of fish, the number in the sea starts to go down. This is called overfishing.

Modern fishing boats make catching fish much easier than it used to be.

Fishermen use helicopters to look for schools of fish.

Fishing controls

Some countries try to control the problem of overfishing. They make fishermen use special nets which only catch the larger fish.

The big holes in this fishing net allow small fish to escape.

Fish in danger

These fish are all in danger from overfishing. If fishermen don't stop catching them soon, they will die out completely.

Up to 70 million sharks are caught each year. Their fins are used to make soup. The rest is thrown away.

Small fish, such as haddock, are overfished.

Cod can grow up to 1.5m (5ft) long, but there are almost no big cod left, because of overfishing.

Pacific salmon have been overfished.

Millions of bigeye tuna are caught each year to make a Japanese food called sushi.

Coral in danger

Coral reefs are being damaged all over the world. Reefs grow slowly. Every reef that people damage will take hundreds of years to grow again.

★ Fishermen use poison to catch tropical fish from reefs. They sell them to pet shops.

People take coral to make things such as necklaces.

Coral is often damaged by careless divers.

Getting warmer

Many scientists think the Earth's temperature is slowly rising. As it gets warmer, the sea level will rise. The ocean currents and weather patterns may also change.

Trapped heat

The Earth is surrounded by a blanket of gases called the atmosphere. Some of these, called greenhouse gases, trap heat around the Earth, making it warm enough for life to exist. But people do some things that make extra gases. These trap more heat, so the Earth and its oceans get warmer.

The Sun's rays warm the Earth. Some of the heat escapes back into space.

Greenhouse gases in the atmosphere stop some of the heat from escaping.

Power stations give off greenhouse gases as they burn coal and oil to make electricity.

Greenhouse gases are made when forests are burned to clear land for farming and building.

Piles of rotting waste give off greenhouse gases.

This picture shows some of the things that people do which can make more greenhouse gases.

Cars burn fuel and produce exhaust fumes, which add more greenhouse gases to the atmosphere.

★ Atmosphere (shown here in blue)

Melting ice

As the atmosphere warms up, the ice in the Arctic and the Antarctic starts to melt. When free-floating sea ice melts, it only makes a slight difference to the sea level. This is because it is made of fresh water, which is less dense than salty sea water.

The air gets warmer.

Ice melts into the sea.

Rising seas

If the world's land ice melted, it would cause a worldwide disaster. The sea level everywhere would rise by more than 60m (200ft). To stop this from happening, we need to find ways of making energy without burning fuels such as oil and coal. Find out more on the next page.

This picture shows what would happen to a town by the sea if the sea level rose by 60m (200ft).

Many islands in the sea would be flooded if all the ice melted.

Internet links

For links to websites where you can play games and learn about global warming, go to **www.usborne-quicklinks.com** and enter the keywords "first seas".

As ice melts at the poles, huge chunks of it fall into the sea.

The future of the oceans

Fuels, such as oil, may one day run out, and anyway, using them harms the Earth. But there are ways of getting energy from the sea itself. In the future, we could get most of our energy from the sea, and even live in it.

Wind power

The surface of the sea is often windy. Big windmills, called wind turbines, could be attached to the seabed and used to make electricity from the wind.

Seabed

Wind blowing across the sea turns the windmill blades.

The spinning blades power a machine called a turbine inside the windmill, which makes electricity.

Water power

This bridge in France is also a power station. It is built across an estuary (a place where a river meets the sea). As the tide comes in and out it turns wheels under the water, which make electricity.

Bridge

Turbine ★ blades turn, making electricity.

Water flows in.

This cutaway picture shows how the power station works.

Living undersea

In the future, people could live in the oceans. A diver named Jacques Cousteau did some experiments in the 1960s, which showed that living under the sea was possible.

Kelp grows very quickly. People living undersea could farm it for food.

This is a picture of what an undersea village might look like.

People could enter their houses from the bottom.

Bars outside the entrances to undersea houses could keep out dangerous animals.

Internet links

For links to websites where you can find out more about the future of the oceans, go to **www.usborne-quicklinks.com**.

Undersea facts and records

The sea animals with the biggest eyes are giant squid. Their eyes are the size of basketballs.

Giant kelp are the fastest growing plants in the world. They grow up to 60cm (24in) each day.

The biggest coral reef in the world is the Great Barrier Reef off the east coast of Australia. It is so big, that it can be seen from space.

The slowest swimming sea creature is the dwarf seahorse. It would take one 2 days to swim 1km (½ mile).

The fastest fish in the sea is the sailfish. It can swim at incredible speeds of up to 110kph (70mph).

The smallest fish in the sea is the dwarf goby. A fully-grown dwarf goby is less than 1cm (½ in) long.

Pacific giant octopuses can grow to enormous sizes. The tentacles of a fully-grown giant octopus can measure over 2m (7ft) long.

Blue whales are the biggest animals that have ever lived. They grow up to 33m (110ft) long. That's longer than a tennis court.

Dolphins have amazing hearing. They hear sounds through a special bone in their lower jaw.

Box jellyfish have deadly poisonous tentacles. Their poison could kill a person in under 4 minutes.

Emperor penguins are excellent swimmers and can stay underwater for up to 18 minutes.

Diatoms are a kind of plankton. Their shells are used to make dynamite.

Killer whales are black on top so that prey swimming above them can't see them against the dark depths.

Flying fish escape from predators by jumping out of the sea. They can glide for over 1km (½ mile).

Pufferfish contain a deadly poison called tetradetoxin. One drop of tetradetoxin could kill a person.

Average sizes

★
Giant octopus 2m (7ft) long

★
Dolphin 2.5m (8ft) long

★
Killer whale 7m (23ft) long

★
Giant squid 18m (60ft) long

★
Blue whale 30m (99ft) long

Index

abalone shells, 51
anemones, 13, 16
     strawberry, 41
Antarctic Ocean, *see* Southern Ocean
arches, 39
Arctic Ocean, 5, 32, 57
artifacts, 49
Atlantic Ocean, 5

bacteria, 9
barnacles, 25, 41
beaches, 38
boats, 44, 45
brittle stars, 12

camouflage, 10, 11
caves, 39
clams, giant, 13
cliffs, 39
coal, 56, 57
coasts, 4, 38, 39
coelacanths, 47
cone shells, 18
corals, 12, 13
     brain, 12
coral animals, 12, 13, 14,15
coral reefs, 6, 12, 13, 14, 15, 17,
     55, 60
crabs, 40
     hermit, 41
     horseshoe, 51
crinoids, 29
crittercams, 46
cruise ships, 44, 45
currents, 36
cuttlebones, 37
cuttlefish, 11, 37

Deep Flight submersible, 46
divers, 4, 20, 23, 48, 55
dog whelks, 41
dolphins, 6, 26, 27, 61
     bottlenose, 27
     spinner, 27

earthquakes, 43

eels, 12
     elvers, 31
     freshwater, 31
     gulper, 28
     moray, 17, 48
estuaries, 58

feather stars, 13
fish, 7
     angelfish, 12, 14
     anglerfish, 29
     bigeye tuna, 55
     blennies, 40
     boxfish, 15
     butterfish, 40
     butterfly fish, 15
     cleanerfish, 17
     clownfish, 16
     clown triggerfish, 14
     cod, 55
     coelacanths, 47
     crescent-tailed bigeye fish, 15
     dwarf gobies, 60
     five-bearded rocklings, 40
     flashlight fish, 29
     flying fish, 61
     gobies, 17
     groupers, 17
        giant, 14
     haddock, 55
     hatchetfish, 28
     herring, 9
     icefish, Antarctic, 32
     lanternfish, 29
     lionfish, 18
     mackerel, 8, 9
     oarfish, 47
     parrotfish, 13
     pearlfish, 16
     pufferfish, 15, 61
     rabbitfish, 18
     remoras, 16
     sailfish, 60
     salmon, 31
        Pacific, 55
     sargassum frogfish, 11

sea scorpions, 41
shrimpfish, 11
stonefish, 18
tuna, 9
viperfish, 29
fishermen, 50, 55
fishing nets, 50

galleons, 44
galleys, 44
giant clams, 13
giant kelp, 60
giant squid, 47, 60, 61
Great Barrier Reef, 60

headlands, 39
helicopters, 54
hovercraft, 45
hurricanes, 42, 43

Indian Ocean, 5
islands, 5

jellyfish,
        box, 18, 61
        porpita, 19

kelp, 59, 60

limpets, 41
living undersea, 59

Mariana Trench, 5
mermaid's purse, 37
migration, 30
mother-of-pearl, 51
mussels, 40

nutrients, 9

octopuses, 14
        blue-ringed, 18
        Pacific giant, 60, 61
oil, 4, 51, 53, 56, 57, 58
oil platforms, 4, 51
oil tankers, 45, 53
overfishing, 54, 55

Pacific Ocean, 5
pearls, 51

penguins, 33
        emperor, 33, 61
Petronas Towers, 5
plankton, 8, 23, 30
        copepods, 30
        diatoms, 8, 61
        phytoplankton, 8, 9
        zooplankton, 8, 9
poison, 6, 18, 19, 55
Portuguese man-of-war, 18
power stations, 56, 58

rays, 22, 23
        electric, 22
        manta, 22, 23
        stingrays, 22

sailing ships, 44
salmon, 31
        Pacific, 55
Santa Margerita, 49
Sargasso Sea, 31
schools, 15
seabed, 4
seabirds, 53
        seagulls, 37
seahorses, 14
        dwarf, 60
seals, 32, 53
seaweed, 11, 37, 40, 41, 51, 59
        sargassum, 11
sea dragons, 10
sea fans, 12
sea lemons, 41
sea level, 37, 56, 57
sea slugs, 6, 19
sea snakes, 19
sea urchins, 11, 12, 41
sewage, 52
sharks, 19, 20, 21, 55
        great white, 20
        hammerhead, 21
        megamouth, 47
        sand tiger, 21
        whale, 21
        wobbegong, 10
shipwrecks, 48
shrimps, 17, 40
        banded coral, 17
Southern Ocean, 5, 32, 57

sponges, 12
squid
      giant, 47, 60, 61
      vampire, 28
starfish, 41
storms, 42
submersibles, 46
symbiosis, 16

tideline, 37
tides, 37, 58
Titanic, 49
treasure, 49
tsunami, 43

turtles, 16, 31
volcanoes, 5

walruses, 32
waterspouts, 42
waves, 34
whales, 24, 25, 30
      blue, 24, 60, 61
      humpback, 9, 24, 25, 30
      killer, 8, 9, 61
      minke, 24
      right, 24
      sperm, 24, 25, 46
wind turbines, 58

Acknowledgements

The publishers are grateful to the following for permission to reproduce material:

Key: t = top, m = middle, b = bottom, l = left, r = right

Alamy: Cover spine © JL Images/Alamy, 12tr © Vova Pomortzeff/Alamy. Ardea London: 6ml, 24-25t © Francois Gohier/ardea.com, 10b © Kevin Deacon/Auscape/ardea.com, 47mr © Peter J.Green/ardea.com, 61tm © Valerie Taylor/ardea.com. Bruce Coleman Collection: 1b © Richard Herman/Innerspace Visions, 6t, 15tl, 18tr, 26tl © Pacific Stock/Bruce Coleman, 25bl © Johnny Johnson/Bruce Coleman, 32b © Hans Reinhard/ Bruce Coleman. Corbis: 5b © Steve Raymer/Corbis, 8tl © Amos Nachoum/Corbis, 8bl © Douglas P. Wilson/Frank Lane Picture Agency/Corbis, 8br, 61ml © Douglas P. Wilson/Frank Lane Picture Agency/Corbis, 14tl © Tom Brakefield/Corbis, 14ml © Robert Yin/Corbis, 16t © Lawson Wood/Corbis, 19b, 21br © Brandon D. Cole/Corbis, 20-21 © Jeffrey.L.Rotman/Corbis, 20bl © Stuart Westmorland/Corbis, 34ml © Gary Braasch/Corbis, 42 © Bettmann/Corbis, 45bl © Craig Aurness/Corbis, 45br © Dean Conger/Corbis, 49tr, 49mr © Jonathan Blair/Corbis, 49br © Ralph White/Corbis, 52tr © Ian Harwood/Ecoscene/Corbis, 53bl © George D. Lepp/Corbis, 55tl © Amos Nachoum/Corbis, 58b © Yann Arthus-Bertrand/Corbis, 61m © Stephen Frink/Corbis. Digital Vision: Back cover, 3br, 26tl, 30m, 35b, 38br, 55r, 57b, 60t, 61t © Digital Vision. Getty Images: Cover © David Nardini/Getty Images, 6bl © Georgette Douwma/Photographer's Choice/Getty Images, 6br © David Doubilet/National Geographic/Getty Images. Imagequest 3-D: 19m © Peter Parks/imagequestmarine.com. Naturepl: 30br © Sinclair Stammers/naturepl.com, 47r © Bruce Rasner/Jeff Rotman/naturepl.com, 60m, 60bl © Jeff Rotman/Avi Klapfer/naturepl.com, 60r © David Hall/naturepl.com, 61r © Hans Christoph Kappel/naturepl.com. NOAA: 42l © NOAA. Oxford Scientific Films: 31cl © Roger Jackman/Oxford Scientific Film/photolibrary. com. Philip Colla: 21tr © Philip Colla. Photoshot: 14m © Yves Lanceau/Photoshot, 16bl © Reinhard Dirscherl/Oceans-Image/Photoshot, 46tr © Norbert Wu/Photoshot, 55l © Jeff Goodman/Photoshot, 55tc © Kevin Schafer/Photoshot, 60cl © B Jones & M Shimlock/Photoshot. Powerstock Zefa Ltd: 31b © Powerstock Zefa. Popperfoto: 53bl © Daniel Joubert/Popperfoto. Rudolf Svensen: 55tc © Rudolf Svensen. Specialist stock: 22bl © Wolfgang Poelzer/WaterFrame/Still Pictures, 23m © Franco Banfi/WaterFrame/Still Pictures, 27ml © Horst Schafer/Peter Arnold/Specialist Stock, 30tr © Yves Lefevre/Bios/Specialist Stock, 30br © Biosphoto/Lecomte Jean/BIOSphoto/Still Pictures, 31bl (Roland Birke), 50-51 © Mike Schroeder/Argus/Specialist Stock.

Additional Illustrators: Ian Jackson, John Woodcock, Chris Shields.
Digital manipulation: John Russell. Cover Design: Stephen Moncrieff.

The publishers would like to thank Hawkes Ocean Technologies (H.O.T.) for their permission to feature the Deep Flight Submersible in this book. Special thanks to Bob Whiteaker, for help with the diagrams.

Every effort has been made to trace and acknowledge ownership of copyright. If any rights have been omitted, the publishers offer to rectify this in any subsequent editions following notification.